Banks

Published in the United States of America by Cherry Lake Publishing
Ann Arbor, Michigan
www.cherrylakepublishing.com

Content Adviser: Danielle Peart, CPA
Reading Adviser: Cecilia Minden, PhD, Literacy expert and children's author
Book Design: Jennifer Wahi
Illustrator: Jeff Bane

Photo Credits: © Andrey_Popov/Shutterstock.com, 5; © vetkit/Shutterstock.com, 7; © ImageFlow/Shutterstock.com, 9; © djile/Shutterstock.com, 11; © Monkey Business Images/Shutterstock.com, 13; © Rawpixel.com/Shutterstock.com, 15; © Syda Productions/Shutterstock.com, 17; © Hadrian/Shutterstock.com, 19; © SEKr/Shutterstock.com, 21; © Corepics VOF/Shutterstock.com, 23; Cover, 1, 6, 12, 14, Jeff Bane

Library of Congress Cataloging-in-Publication Data

Names: Colby, Jennifer, 1971- author.
Title: Banks / Jennifer Colby.
Description: Ann Arbor : Cherry Lake Publishing, [2018] | Series: My guide to money | Includes bibliographical references and index.
Identifiers: LCCN 2018003330| ISBN 9781534129023 (hardcover) | ISBN 9781534130722 (pdf) | ISBN 9781534132221 (pbk.) | ISBN 9781534133921 (hosted ebook)
Subjects: LCSH: Banks and banking--Juvenile literature.
Classification: LCC HG1609 .C65 2018 | DDC 332.1--dc23
LC record available at https://lccn.loc.gov/2018003330

Printed in the United States of America
Corporate Graphics

About the author: Jennifer Colby is a school librarian in Michigan. She keeps her money safe at the bank.

About the illustrator: Jeff Bane and his two business partners own a studio along the American River in Folsom, California, home of the 1849 Gold Rush. When Jeff's not sketching or illustrating for clients, he's either swimming or kayaking in the river to relax.

Do you have a piggy bank?
It keeps money safe.

But there are safer places to keep money.

Banks keep money safe.

You can open up different **accounts** at a bank.

What do you save money for?

You can open up a savings account. People use this to save money. They save for vacations. They save for new clothes.

What do you spend money on?

You can open up a checking account. People use this to spend money.

PLATINUM Credit

⑮

You can put money in your accounts. This is called a deposit. It can go into your savings or checking account.

You can take money out of
your accounts. This is called
a withdrawal. You could do this
at an **ATM**.

Banks can pay **interest**. This makes your money at the bank **earn** money.

Have you been to a bank? Visit one with an adult. Talk with the bank **teller**. Ask about spending and saving. Ask about the different accounts. Ask about interest.

glossary

accounts (uh-KOUNTS) places where you keep your money at a bank

ATM (AY-TEE-EM) a machine that people use to get money from their bank accounts; stands for automatic teller machine

earn (URN) to get

interest (IN-trist) money paid to you by a bank for keeping your savings there

teller (TEL-ur) bank worker whose job is to help customers with their money

index